SPOT THE DIFFERENCE

Season's Greetings
Best Wishes
for
Peace and Prosperity
Happy 2011

The Rechtschaffen Group
UBS Financial Services Inc.
UBS International
1285 Avenue of the Americas, 19th Fl
New York, NY 10019 ◆ Tel (212) 713-3400

Joy

Success

Happiness

Now More Than Ever

SPOT THE DIFFERENCE

OVER 100 FANTASTIC PHOTOGRAPHIC PUZZLES

CHARTWELL
BOOKS, INC.

This edition printed in 2010 by
CHARTWELL BOOKS, INC.
A Division of **BOOK SALES, INC.**
276 Fifth Avenue Suite 206
New York, New York 10001 USA

Copyright © 2010 Arcturus Publishing Limited
26/27 Bickels Yard, 151–153 Bermondsey Street,
London SE1 3HA

ISBN-13: 978-0-7858-2683-5
ISBN-10: 0-7858-2683-1
AD001531EN

Printed in Singapore

SPOT THE DIFFERENCE

Attention to detail is often said to be lacking in the modern, bustling world in which we live. Have you an eye for detail? Just how good will you prove to be at spotting when something is different? These pictures will test your powers of observation to the limit.

The puzzles range through five levels of observation, from Warm-Up to Expert, with the numbers of eyes indicating the difficulty levels: we reckon you'll need more than one pair for some of these intricate photos!

If you enjoy the stimulus of working against the clock, then we can give you target times:

⌛ Puzzles in the Warm-Up section should take no more than five minutes to solve

⌛ Standard puzzles should take anywhere between six to eight minutes

⌛ Challenging puzzles between seven and nine minutes

⌛ Tough puzzles about ten minutes

⌛ Expert puzzles may take ten to fifteen minutes each

If you can solve any of these puzzles in less time than recommended, then you really are observant.

In addition, there are puzzles which challenge you to spot just one difference, or to spot where things are hidden or missing; there are also reflected pictures, 'spot the same', negatives, and many other picture puzzles to provide variety, and to add to your puzzling pleasure.

Tick off the changes as you find them, then check to see if you are right, by turning to the solutions at the back of the book.

CONTENTS

EXAMPLE

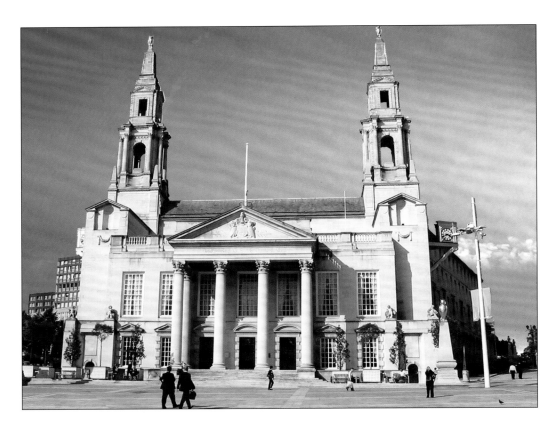

1 2 3 4 5 6 7 8

PUZZLES

CHINESE FISHERMAN

1 2 3 4 5 6 7 8

CORKS

1   2   3   4   5   6   7   8

ONE DIFFERENCE EACH

SPOT THE ORNAMENTS

Of the six scenes below, which is the only one to appear in the picture above?

ORANGE BIKE

1   2   3   4   5   6   7   8

TROPICAL DRINKS

TROPICAL DRINKS

1 2 3 4 5 6 7 8

1   2   3   4   5   6   7   8   9   10

HAVING A GOOD TIME

| 1 | 2 | 3 | 4 | 5 | 6 | 7 | 8 |

BABY COOK

1 2 3 4 5 6 7 8

A MODERN HOUSE

1   2   3   4   5   6   7   8

11

1   2   3   4   5   6   7   8

1 2 3 4 5 6 7 8

ORIENTAL GARDEN

ORIENTAL GARDEN

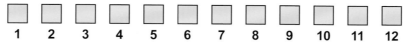

1 2 3 4 5 6 7 8 9 10 11 12

TROPICAL FRUIT

| 1 | 2 | 3 | 4 | 5 | 6 | 7 | 8 |

HIDDEN FISH

The six fish below have all been hidden in the picture above.
Can you spot them hiding in the water?

1 2 3 4 5 6 7 8

MARCHING BAND

1	2	3	4	5	6	7	8

STRAW HATS

1 2 3 4 5 6 7 8

TOTEM POLE

DISCO LIGHTS

DISCO LIGHTS

PAMPER YOURSELF

1 2 3 4 5 6 7 8

WRISTWATCH

1 2 3 4 5 6 7 8

FIREWORKS

FIREWORKS

☐ ☐ ☐ ☐ ☐ ☐ ☐ ☐
1　2　3　4　5　6　7　8

VEGETABLES

| 1 | 2 | 3 | 4 | 5 | 6 | 7 | 8 | 9 | 10 |

SNOWBOARDERS

☐ ☐ ☐ ☐ ☐ ☐ ☐ ☐ ☐ ☐
1   2   3   4   5   6   7   8   9   10

KOREAN CARVINGS

| 1 | 2 | 3 | 4 | 5 | 6 | 7 | 8 |

| 1 | 2 | 3 | 4 | 5 | 6 | 7 | 8 |

BIG WIGS

BIG WIGS

GLASS ANIMALS

GLASS ANIMALS

SHOES

☐ ☐ ☐ ☐ ☐ ☐ ☐ ☐
1　2　3　4　5　6　7　8

THE CAMEL

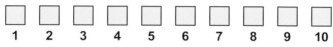

| 1 | 2 | 3 | 4 | 5 | 6 | 7 | 8 | 9 | 10 |

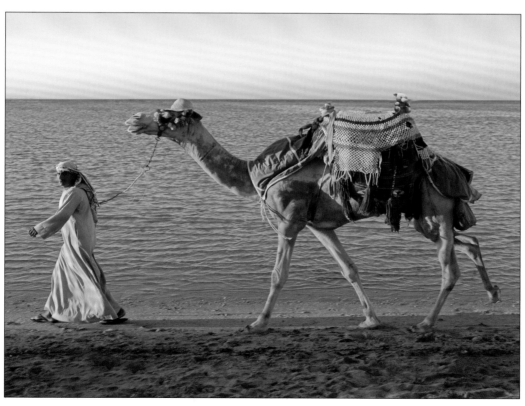

BROKEN TOYS

BROKEN TOYS

| 1 | 2 | 3 | 4 | 5 | 6 | 7 | 8 |

HIDDEN bugs

The six bugs below have all been hidden in the picture above.
Can you spot them hiding in the lichen?

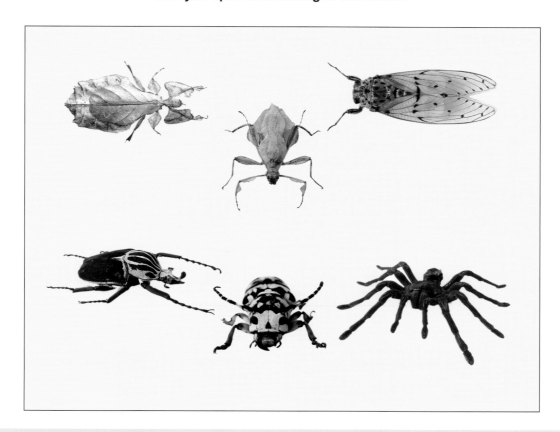

MASKS

MASKS

ALL DRESSED UP

ALL DRESSED UP

ENGINE PARTS

In which order should the twelve pictures above be placed,
in order to create an exact copy of the picture below?

SUNBATHERS

38

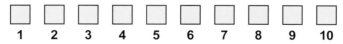

| 1 | 2 | 3 | 4 | 5 | 6 | 7 | 8 | 9 | 10 |

ONE DIFFERENCE

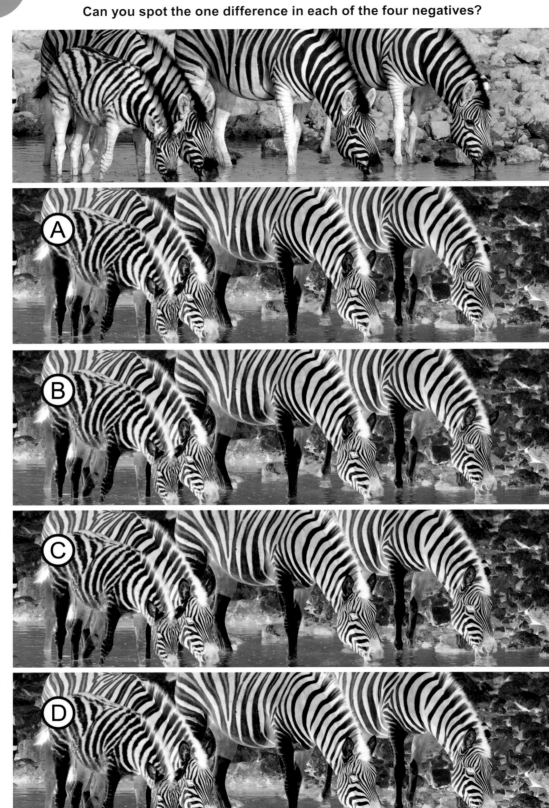

39

Can you spot the one difference in each of the four negatives?

A 1

B 1

C 1

D 1

DOLLS' HEADS

LAKESIDE

LAKESIDE

MOSCOW OPERA HOUSE

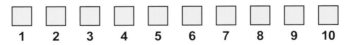

| 1 | 2 | 3 | 4 | 5 | 6 | 7 | 8 | 9 | 10 |

GEOGRAPHY LESSON

JIGSAW PUZZLE

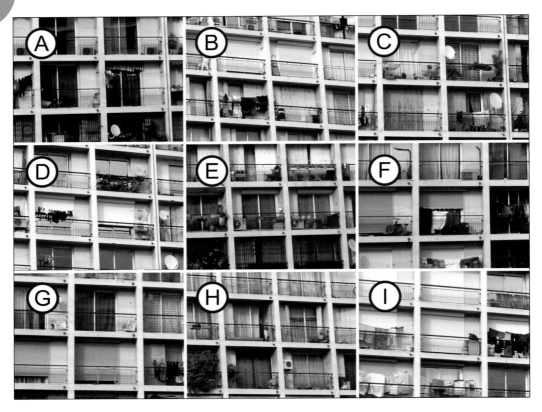

In which order should the nine pictures above be placed,
in order to create an exact copy of the picture below?

CLOTHES SHOP

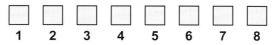

1   2   3   4   5   6   7   8

HAPPY ARTISTS

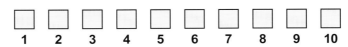

| 1 | 2 | 3 | 4 | 5 | 6 | 7 | 8 | 9 | 10 |

1 2 3 4 5 6 7 8

CHEESE SELECTION

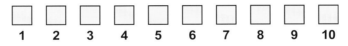

| 1 | 2 | 3 | 4 | 5 | 6 | 7 | 8 | 9 | 10 |

SPOT THE BEE

□
1

TRENDY LOFT

TRENDY LOFT

WOODEN SHOES

WOODEN SHOES

☐ ☐ ☐ ☐ ☐ ☐ ☐ ☐ ☐ ☐ ☐ ☐
1 2 3 4 5 6 7 8 9 10 11 12

DIVING

1   2   3   4   5   6   7   8   9   10

SEAFOOD

1   2   3   4   5   6   7   8

CITY HALL

CITY HALL

☐ ☐ ☐ ☐ ☐ ☐ ☐ ☐ ☐ ☐ ☐ ☐
1   2   3   4   5   6   7   8   9   10   11   12

ONE DIFFERENCE

Can you spot the one difference in each of the five negatives?

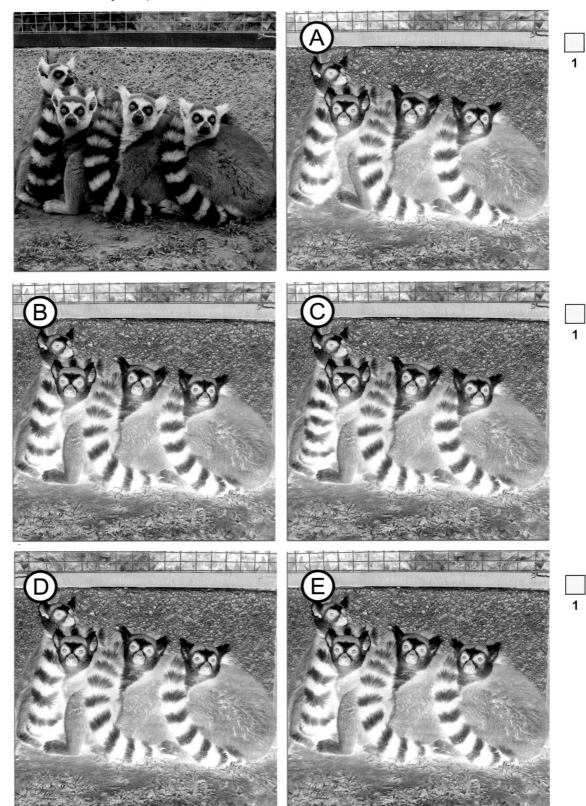

MACHU PICCHU

☆ ☆ ☆

| | | | | | | | | | |
|1|2|3|4|5|6|7|8|9|10|

KITCHEN

1 2 3 4 5 6 7 8 9 10

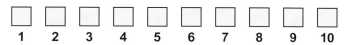

1 2 3 4 5 6 7 8 9 10

CRUMBLY BUILDING

CRUMBLY BUILDING

☐ ☐ ☐ ☐ ☐ ☐ ☐ ☐ ☐ ☐
1 2 3 4 5 6 7 8 9 10

SEWING KIT

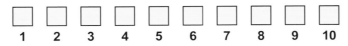

| 1 | 2 | 3 | 4 | 5 | 6 | 7 | 8 | 9 | 10 |

FUNFAIR

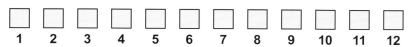

| 1 | 2 | 3 | 4 | 5 | 6 | 7 | 8 | 9 | 10 | 11 | 12 |

CUTTING OUT

CUTTING OUT

Of the six clips below, which is the only one to appear in the picture opposite?

THE CASTLE

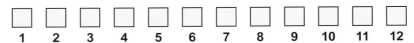

| 1 | 2 | 3 | 4 | 5 | 6 | 7 | 8 | 9 | 10 | 11 | 12 |

TIME FOR LUNCH

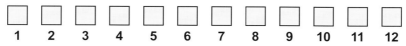

1   2   3   4   5   6   7   8   9   10   11   12

RUSSIAN DOLLS

| 1 | 2 | 3 | 4 | 5 | 6 | 7 | 8 | 9 |

TRAIN STATION

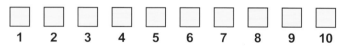

1 2 3 4 5 6 7 8 9 10

HENNAED HANDS

□ □ □ □ □ □ □ □ □ □ □ □
1 2 3 4 5 6 7 8 9 10 11 12

HIEROGLYPHICS

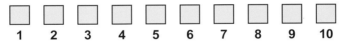

1   2   3   4   5   6   7   8   9   10

PANEL IN REFLECTION

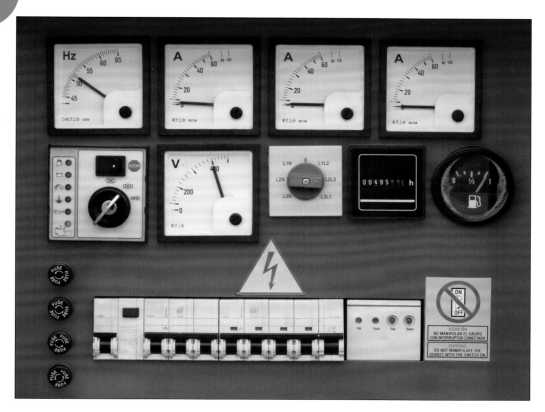

| 1 | 2 | 3 | 4 | 5 | 6 | 7 | 8 |

SHADOW PUPPETS

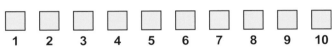

CHAMELEON

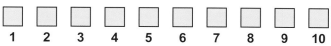

1	2	3	4	5	6	7	8	9	10

CHRISTMAS GIFTS

☐ ☐ ☐ ☐ ☐ ☐ ☐ ☐ ☐ ☐
1　2　3　4　5　6　7　8　9　10

WINDMILLS

WINDMILLS

1 2 3 4 5 6 7 8 9 10 11 12

FRUIT

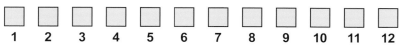

1   2   3   4   5   6   7   8   9   10   11   12

CHRISTMAS LIGHTS

CHRISTMAS LIGHTS

| 1 | 2 | 3 | 4 | 5 | 6 | 7 | 8 | 9 | 10 | 11 | 12 | 13 | 14 |

CLOTH ANIMALS

CLOTH ANIMALS

JIGSAW PUZZLE

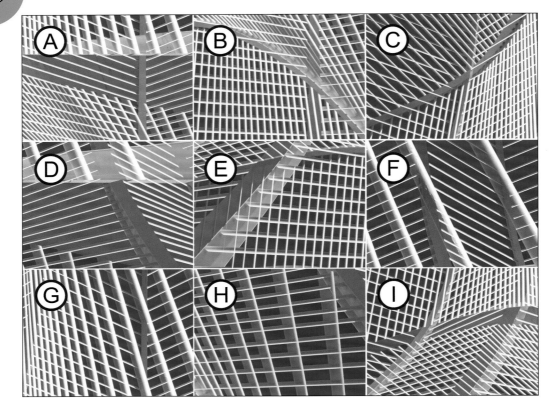

In which order should the twelve pictures above be placed,
in order to create an exact copy of the picture below?

HARBOUR SCENE

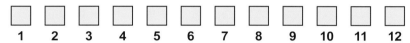

1 2 3 4 5 6 7 8 9 10 11 12

HOUSES ON A HILL

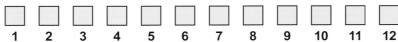

1 2 3 4 5 6 7 8 9 10 11 12

MOSAIC

81

1   2   3   4   5   6   7   8   9   10   11   12

CUTTING OUT

CUTTING OUT

Of the six clips below, which is the only one to appear in the picture opposite?

VENETIAN MASKS

| 1 | 2 | 3 | 4 | 5 | 6 | 7 | 8 | 9 | 10 |

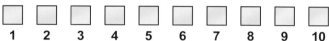

1   2   3   4   5   6   7   8   9   10

NATIVE SHIELDS

NATIVE SHIELDS

☐ ☐ ☐ ☐ ☐ ☐ ☐ ☐ ☐ ☐ ☐ ☐
1　2　3　4　5　6　7　8　9　10　11　12

STREET PROCESSION

STREET PROCESSION

☐ ☐ ☐ ☐ ☐ ☐ ☐ ☐ ☐ ☐ ☐ ☐
1 2 3 4 5 6 7 8 9 10 11 12

117

CIRCLES IN REFLECTION

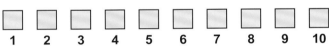

1 2 3 4 5 6 7 8 9 10

CHEMICAL PLANT

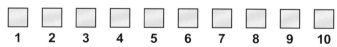

1 2 3 4 5 6 7 8 9 10

BOWLS

1   2   3   4   5   6   7   8   9   10

BREAD

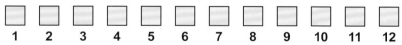

1	2	3	4	5	6	7	8	9	10	11	12

PAINTED CEILING

PAINTED CEILING

☐ 1 ☐ 2 ☐ 3 ☐ 4 ☐ 5 ☐ 6 ☐ 7 ☐ 8 ☐ 9 ☐ 10 ☐ 11 ☐ 12 ☐ 13 ☐ 14

DRESS IN REFLECTION

DRESS IN REFLECTION

TOTEM POLES

TOTEM POLES

ONE DIFFERENCE EACH

1 2 3 4 5 6 7 8 9 10 11 12

BEADS IN REFLECTION

| 1 | 2 | 3 | 4 | 5 | 6 | 7 | 8 | 9 | 10 |

JAPANESE DOLLS

1 2 3 4 5 6 7 8 9 10 11 12 13 14

WALKING IN THE SNOW

WALKING IN THE SNOW

ISTANBUL

ISTANBUL

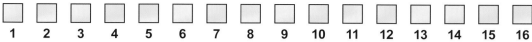

1 2 3 4 5 6 7 8 9 10 11 12 13 14 15 16

WEB IN REFLECTION

1 2 3 4 5 6 7 8 9 10

SOLUTIONS

1

2

3

4

5

6

7

8

9

10

11

12

13

14

15

16

17

18

20

19

21

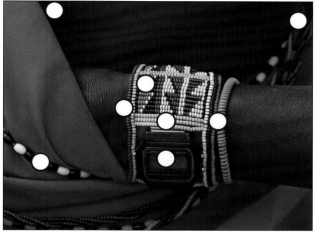

22

23

24

25

26

27

28

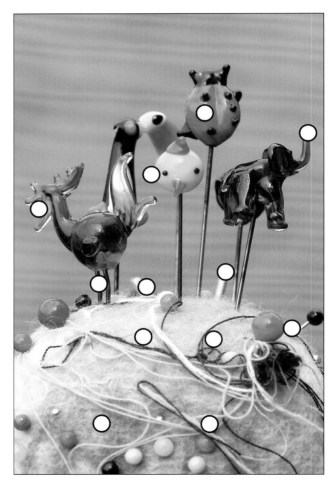

29

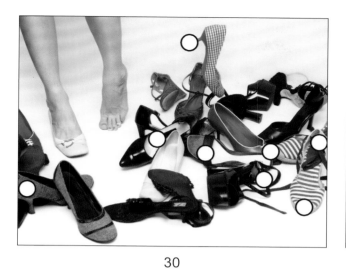

30

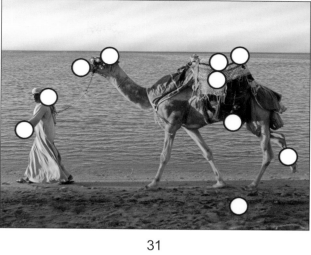

31

32

33

34

35

36

37

38

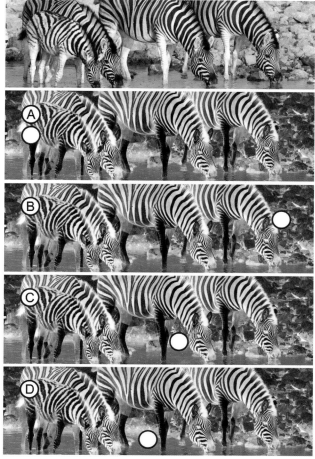

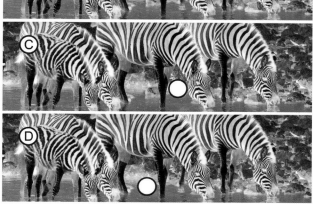

39

40

41

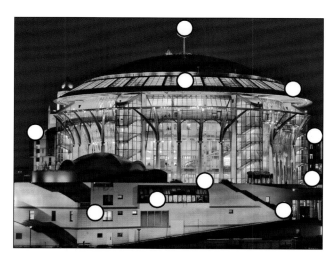

42

43

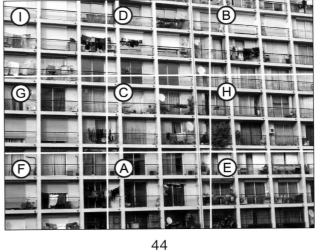

44

45

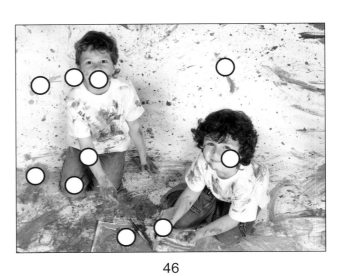

46

47

48

49

50

51

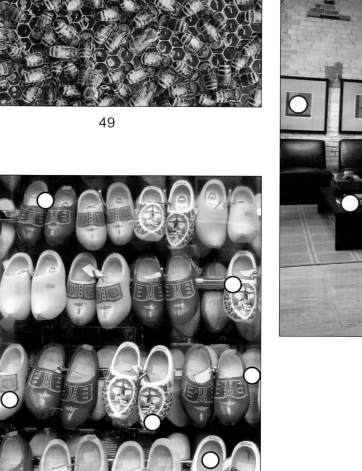

52

53

54

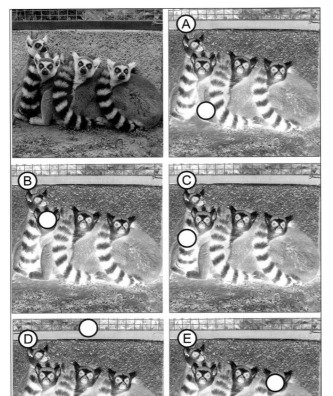

55

56

57

58

59

60

61

62

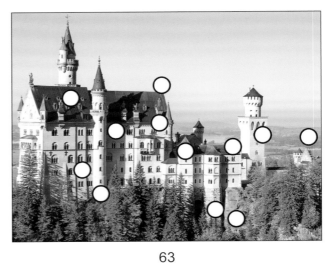

63

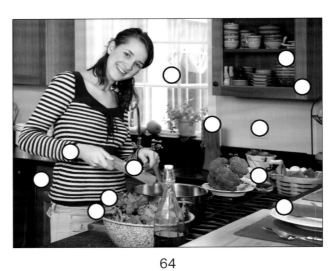

64

65

66

67

68

69

70

71

72

73

74

75

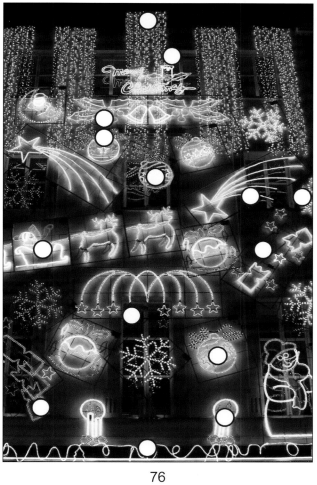

76

77

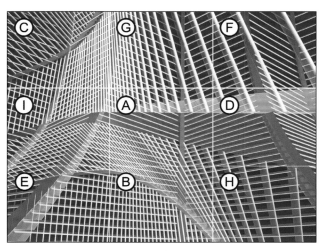

78

79

155

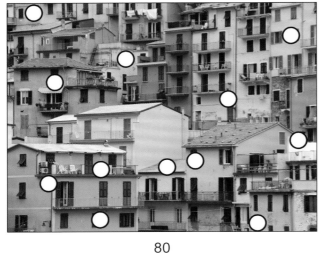

80

81

82

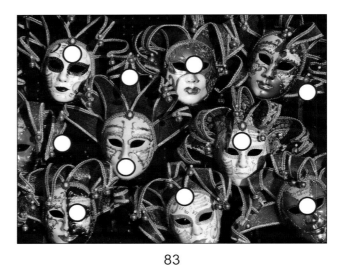

83

84

85

86

87

88

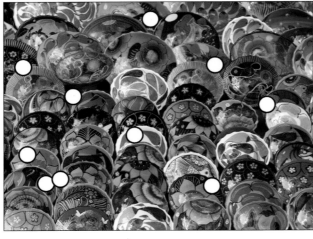

89

90

91

92

93

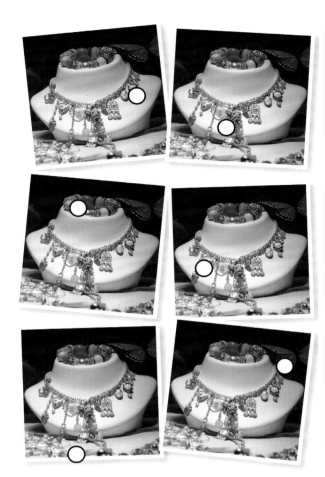

94

95

96

97

98

99

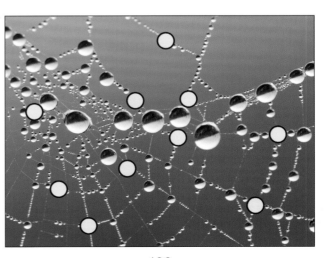

100